Internet Searches Guidebook

By Daniel Farb, M.D., and Bruce Gordon

Please send any correspondence regarding permissions to:
UniversityOfHealthCare
419 N. Larchmont Blvd., #323
Los Angeles, CA 90004

Internet Searches Guidebook

ISBN: 1594912718

Library of Congress Catalog Number: 2005927140

UniversityOfHealthCare website: www.uohc.com

Neither the author nor the publisher assumes any liability for the information contained in this title. Every reader must consult the latest professional information available at the time and employ it in consultation with a professional who is familiar with the specific situation.

Contents

Introduction

This book is a text-only version of the CD product with the same name. We have made it for those who prefer books. However, we have tried to retain the flavor of the CD approach. You can find review questions scattered throughout the book. Cases and examples taken from the CD are included.

About the Authors

M. Daniel Farb, CEO of UniversityOfHealthCare and UniversityOfBusiness, is a leader in the field of interactive management and healthcare e-learning. He received a BA in English Literature from Yale (where he set an academic record and studied with writers like Robert Penn Warren), an M.D. from Boston University, a degree in Executive Management from the Anderson School of Business at UCLA, and is currently working on a degree at UCLA in International Trade. He is a practicing ophthalmologist. He also has received two patents in ophthalmology and is working on others, has worked with the World Health Organization in Geneva and the National Institutes of Health in Washington, D.C. He has written scientific and popular articles, and has worked as a newspaper reporter. He helped Dr. Robbins edit one of the editions of Robbins' "Pathology" textbook for readability. He wrote an article on humor for the Massachusetts Review. He has experience in theater and television, including acting, directing, and stage-managing. He has programmed his own patient records database. He has written and edited hundreds of e-learning courses.

Dr. Farb is a member of the American Academy of Ophthalmology, the Union of American Physicians and Dentists, the AOJS, the American Association of Physicians and Surgeons, the ASTD (American Society for Training and Development), the E-Learning Forum, the Southern California Biomedical Council, the PDA (Parenteral Drug Association), and the Medical Marketing Association.

Bruce Gordon is the Creative Director for UniversityOfHealthCare, LLC, and plays an important role in writing the more creative projects, especially those with stories.

After receiving a BA in Economics from UCLA, he began a freelance writing career that included technical writing (such as a manual for Princess Cruise Lines), stand-up comedy routines for nationally known comedians, and screenplay writing. He has done production support work with famous Hollywood personalities on such well-known productions as Aaron Spelling's "Dynasty" and "Love Boat" TV shows.

An audio-visual software specialist, he is a versatile artist, with published works in a variety of media, including music, motion graphics, and digital video short film.

INTERNET SEARCHES

Objectives

This title is designed to assist you in learning how to use the Internet to search for information. Although it is geared toward sales and marketing in the health care professions, the techniques and services described are applicable to finding information on virtually any topic.

Please be aware that the information contained herein is current at the time of this writing. Sites and services change frequently and/or may still show content that has been outdated. It is the very nature of the Internet to change and update information constantly. Web page revisions and changes of Web Addresses should be considered the norm.

SEARCH OVERVIEW

One can find everything on the Internet:
- Weather
- Stock market quotes
- Late-breaking news
- Online textbooks
- Encyclopedias
- Databases

Whereas users previously went to libraries to research a topic using print sources such as textbooks and indexes, they now can search online from the comfort of their own homes or offices, or they can go to the library to "surf the Net."

One of the strengths of the Net is the fact that it allows immediate access to current information; yet this leads to major weaknesses. Because the Web has grown at such a rapid pace to millions of pages without any structured regulation, searching for specific items is not easy.

Also, since anyone can publish information on the Web, the searcher must be very careful to evaluate search results before using it. This is especially important in the area of healthcare, where one should consult his or her physicians before assuming the appropriateness of any treatment information located on the Internet. The process of evaluating Web information is covered in detail later.

Commonly-used sites for health care information include professional associations (such as the American Medical Association: (www.ama-assn.org), consumer health sites (such as NOAH: New York Online Access to Health: www.noah.cuny.edu), bibliographic databases (such as MEDLINE via PubMed: www.nlm.nih.gov), medical textbooks (such as Harrison's Online: www.harrisononline.com), and full-text journals (such as APA Monitor Online: www.apa.org/monitor).

It would be helpful enough just to offer an annotated list of recommended Web sites. However, this book seeks to empower you with techniques on how to search efficiently for quality information. All through the book, you will be directed to recommended sites and shown tips on where to start your search through the Web's labyrinth of information.

There will be a series of examples and questions throughout the book. These will feature an orientation toward sales and marketing of drugs for cancer and depression. Another theme in the review questions is the search required to start a LASIK eye surgery center.

A STORY OF MEDICAL INTERNET SEARCHING

Dr. Steven Roberts is opening a cancer center in conjunction with his local hospital, but he's much too busy with his current practice to do all the research involved. So he hires Tanya Adams as a research assistant to find the information for him.

DR. ROBERTS: "I need you to compile a report on starting a business, staffing, competition, statistics, drugs, insurance, managed care, hospital, and other related issues. And I want you to do it the fast and inexpensive way... using Internet resources."

TANYA: "Are you sure I'm the right person for the job? I told you that I'm fairly new to the whole Internet thing."

DR. ROBERTS: "But I know that you're a hard worker and a fast learner. You just need a little coaching, so I'll supply you with the materials of a Medical Internet Search course that I recently took."

TANYA: "Thanks for the vote of confidence. I won't let you down. By the way, what should I look for, specifically?

DR. ROBERTS: "Well, I'd like to learn the demographics of the community, check competition, locate journal articles on cancer care centers, find oncologists in the community, and that sort of thing."

TANYA: "Anything else?"

DR. ROBERTS: "Yes, now that you mention it. I just found out that my uncle has prostate cancer, and I'd like to know the latest treatment procedures. Could you find those too?"

TANYA: "Sure. And since I'll need to work out of your office for high speed Internet access, do you want me to handle your mail?"

DR. ROBERTS: "Yes, thank you. And I'll check in with you periodically to see how things are going. I'll be checking my own e-mail, and I'll send you any new instructions or ideas I come up with while I'm away. You may have to do some of my patient research, too."

TANYA: "With what you're paying? Anything you need!"

DR. ROBERTS: "When can you start?"

TANYA: "Now is as good as any time."

Let's follow along as Tanya learns to search the Internet for medical information.

Search Engines: Definitions and Theory

There are three major categories of search services:
- Engines
- Subject directories
- Metasearch gateways

These distinctions are difficult to make at times because, in the case of engines and directories, a user can browse databases using a hierarchical listing of subject categories. Other terms used to describe these search services are "indexes" and "catalogs."

Search engine services are also called spiders, robots, and crawlers because of their ability to construct a database without using a human as an intermediary. Humans develop the programs that create the database, but the actual locating of content and database construction happens without humans.

Robots visit and revisit content providers, continuously searching for information that should be added, changed, or deleted from their immense databases. These robots have been designed to adhere to strict procedures set up to prevent the resources of the visited server from becoming overwhelmed.

Subject Directories

Subject directories, unlike search engines, are dependent upon human intervention in the search. Humans, frequently librarians, build directory databases, and they analyze Web pages for inclusion or exclusion. With a directory, a user can browse via broad categories often arranged hierarchically-- without having to first enter a keyword.

Yet, just like with pure engines, a directory allows searchers to inquire by keyword.

The databases of directories are usually smaller than those of engines. This is because of the time added to the process by human intervention and the fact that directories have rigid guidelines that sites must meet before being added to their index. Therefore, they have a less sizeable, but cleaner index.

Requests for content are typically made using electronic forms completed by the service offering Web pages or by promotion services such Yahoo! (www.yahoo.com), Galaxy (www.einet.net/galaxy.html), Argus Clearinghouse (www.clearinghouse.net), and Submit It! (www.submit-it.com). Other directories include LookSmart (www.looksmart.com), MSN (www.msn.com), About.com (www.about.com) and Go (www.go.com).

Factors that influence search engine rankings are irrelevant to directory rankings. Since people review sites, more attention is placed on the quality of a site: its functionality, content and design. Directories strive to categorize sites accurately, and they often correct categories suggested by a site's Webmaster. Because the inclusion of directory sites is determined by factors such as payments, subscriptions, advertising arrangements and business partnerships, the search results will be slanted far from general Web search retrievals.

Subject-specific directories are also included in this category. Some of these are: HealthWeb (www.healthweb.org), Medical Matrix (www.medmatrix.org), MedWeb (www.gen.emory.edu/medweb/medweb.html), NOAH (www.noah.cuny.edu), Combined Health Information Database (www.chid.nih.gov), and Healthfinder (www.healthfinder.gov).

An experimental directory, CliniWeb (www.ohsu.edu/cliniweb)), is restricted to clinical content, and it can be browsed by Medical Subject Heading (MeSH).

Directories and engines vary according to search syntax, database size, update frequency, and indexing practices. Directories may actually retrieve better-focused search results, particularly for searchers with less experience. Some directories use external search engines to find links outside the directory's catalog.

A Web directory is kind of like a *Reader's Digest*, filtering and organizing information for you. Directories are easier to use than engines when you need to browse broad subject categories such as news, government, health, etc. Engines usually only deliver good results when supplied with specific, meaningful keywords. Further blurring distinctions among them, however, some search engines have added directories to their search features.

Metasearch Gateways (or Mega Sites)

When a Web site or portal has the ability to query multiple search engines simultaneously or individually using a consistent form, that site is called a metasearch gateway. These sites don't build and index content, so they don't have any database to maintain. The function of a metasearch gateway is to submit search requests to multiple services, then compile and display the results to the searcher, typically on a single page.

However, they have less functionality than individual engines or directory services. Metasearch gateways typically accept simple queries, and then convert them to a common format shared by the aggregated group. But individual search services deal with more complex queries in their own unique manner.

Some well-known portals that query multiple engines simultaneously are:
- MetaCrawler (www.metacrawler.com)
- MetaFind (www.metafind.com)
- Mamma (www.mamma.com)
- Dogpile (www.dogpile.com)
- Inference Find (www.infind.com)
- Internet Sleuth (www.isleuth.com)
- Copernic (www.copernic.com)

Other examples of effective sites that allow fast, simultaneous searching are: The Big Hub (www.thebighub.com), ProFusion (www.profusion.com), and SavvySearch (www.savvysearch.com).

Primarily made up of links to other sites, these portals have little added intellectual value beyond the construction and organization of the links. A metasearch gateway (mega site) acts as a filter to gather the best sites. Many of the best ones organize and annotate the collected sites, typically adding documents of their own.

Megasites let you skip right to the stuff you want. Using them can alleviate the frustration of using multiple search engines to look for relevant information, just to find yourself wading through pages of irrelevant "matches" to find one or two good sites. Even though a good site may be out there, it may not be retrieved by any of the popular engines.

But since the hard work of searching, evaluating, and compiling has already been done for you by qualified professionals, you can prevent getting "garbage" results. This way, if you're looking for organs related to prostate cancer, you won't get pages and pages of pornographic material.

How to Start A Web Search

There is no single correct method to begin a Web search. As a matter of fact, there are as many ways to search for information as there are items of information to be found. Each individual data hunt can have its own best strategy for optimum search results. Once you learn how the different services work, you will be able to make the maximum use of all the available search tools.

Many search services let the user specify what information service he or she wants the information to originate from. For example, a search in Yahoo! can be restricted to one of several delivery mechanisms. Infoseek (now part of Go.com) allows the user to search not only the Web and Usenet but specialized news (PR Newswire, Business Wire, and Reuters) and company information (Hoover's Company Profiles) sources as well.

Browsing

The Web abounds with health information targeted to both health professionals and consumers. It is so saturated with information that just getting started can overwhelm the user. When searching for facts, it's best to start by browsing and gaining comfort with those services that have already cataloged information. Those who have a significant amount of search experience typically start by familiarizing themselves with one of the specialized medical or health subject directories.

Yahoo! Health Information: Web Directories (www.dir.yahoo.com) Health/Web Directories lists over forty of these directories. One example is Hardin Meta Directory of Internet Health Sources (www.lib.uiowa.edu/hardin/md), which is arranged by medical specialty and is a directory of directories.

Also included in the Hardin Meta Directory is the Comprehensive Health and Medical Index (www.lib.uiowa.edu/hardin/md/idx.html) which lists, among other things, reliable directories with established track records for supplying reliable sources of information.

There are other delivery mechanisms, in addition to the Web, that can be browsed. Group discussions in the form of electronic mailing lists and Usenet newsgroups allow users to communicate with others in a group environment.

Usenet Newsgroups

Similar to electronic bulletin boards, Usenet newsgroups are used by people to post information that others can read according to individual preferences. These groups are broken down into broad categories, for example, computers, sports, music, etc. Deja News (www.dejanews.com) has a unique service. It extracts messages from their original groups, reclassifying them into more meaningful divisions. Included under Health is a broad range of topics: Diseases and Disorders, Children's Health, Women's Health, etc.

E-mail Discussion Groups

Lots of people receive regular mass mailings electronically from special interest groups. You have to be a subscriber to the list in order to receive mail. Subscribers and mailings are managed with the utility of software such as LISTSERV, Majordomo, or Listprocessor. A few directories make locating and subscribing to lists of interest easier, e.g. Tile.nct (www.tile.net/lists) and Publicly Accessible Mailing Lists (www.neosoft.com/internet/paml).

Natural Language

Internet search services start off by giving the user a basic form that invites simplicity. Once the searcher enters a query, the service returns search results in a list of pages based on a number of strategies. One of the strategies used by services is to make use of sophisticated statistical algorithms or "fuzzy logic."

Boolean Operators (Applying)

Boolean logic is named after the British mathematician George Boole (1815-1864). Boole designed a system of logic that could produce better search retrievals by formulating precise queries. His term for the system was the "calculus of thought." His writings have led us to derive Boolean logic and its operators:

- AND
- OR
- NOT

These Boolean operators are used to link words and phrases for more precise queries. It is important to note that some search services do not require the uppercase form of Boolean operators, whereas some actually do.

One strategy is to automatically combine the terms and return a list matching any word entered, that is, implied "OR." Yet another strategy is to return a list in which all terms are present, that is, implied "AND." Some engines allow you exclude terms by entering "AND NOT."

All of the major engines and directories enable the searcher to go beyond the simple interface and build more sophisticated search statements that use Boolean and positional operators as well as field searching. By referring to a service's advanced options or help pages, these features are easily located.

There are resources that document and chart the features beyond natural language that services support. One such resource is *Power Searching for Anyone* (www.searchenginewatch.com/facts/powersearch.html) by Danny Sullivan. Another is the *Search Engine Comparison Chart* (www.kcpl.lib.mo.us/search/chart.htm) from the Kansas

City Public Library. These list advanced searching features and how to implement them on different search services.

Alta Vista Example

The next series of pages will familiarize you with the AltaVista search engine and its results pages for Boolean searches using "cancer center," "cancer+center," "cancer AND center," and "cancer AND center AND NOT research."

If you're connected to the Internet, open your browser by clicking www.altavista.com.

Then you can compare your own search with ours.

The best search strategy always demands an individual review of a service's advanced features. It would be virtually impossible to list the preferences of all of the services (some are changing as this is being written). As with other engines and directories, AltaVista offers advanced search options that can be accessed by menus, radio buttons, and drop down lists.

Different search statements and choices will result in quite different results. Some engines and directories require the Boolean "AND," whereas others only respond to "+." Some search services allow the lowercase "and," while others require the uppercase "AND."

View the AltaVista demonstrations of results based on different Boolean entries.
1) cancer center
2) cancer AND center
3) +cancer+center
4) cancer AND center AND NOT research

RESULTS:

Searching Alta Vista for "Cancer Center"

1. OncoLink: A University of Pennsylvania Cancer Center
Resource
Welcome to OncoLink, A University of Pennsylvania Cancer
Center resource. Here you will find in-depth information about
cancer.
URL: oncolink.upenn.edu/
Translate More pages from this site Related pages Facts
about: University Of Pen...

2. Welcome to Wake Forest Comprehensive Cancer Center!
Welcome to the Comprehensive Cancer Center of Wake Forest
University! This site is designed to help you learn more about
the Center, our research...
URL: www.wfubmc.edu/cancer/
Translate Related pages

3. Ohio State University Comprehensive Cancer Center
Research results, the center director's letter, and an academic
calendar are available. View clinical trial details and investigate
its programs.
URL: www-cancer.med.ohio-state.edu/
Translate More pages from this site Related pages Facts
about: Ohio State Univer...

Searching Alta Vista for "+Cancer + Center"
RESULTS:
1. OncoLink: A University of Pennsylvania Cancer Center
Resource

Welcome to OncoLink, A University of Pennsylvania Cancer Center resource. Here you will find in-depth information about cancer.
URL: oncolink.upenn.edu/
Translate More pages from this site Related pages Facts about: University Of Pen...

2. Welcome to Wake Forest Comprehensive Cancer Center! Welcome to the Comprehensive Cancer Center of Wake Forest University! This site is designed to help you learn more about the Center, our research...
URL: www.wfubmc.edu/cancer/
Translate Related pages

3. Ohio State University Comprehensive Cancer Center Research results, the center director's letter, and an academic calendar are available. View clinical trial details and investigate its programs.
URL: www-cancer.med.ohio-state.edu/
Translate More pages from this site Related pages Facts about: Ohio State Univer...

Searching Alta Vista for "Cancer AND Center"
RESULTS
1. NUTRITION AND CANCER
Home | Place an Order. NUTRITION AND CANCER. An International Journal. Editor Leonard A. Cohen CONTRIBUTOR GUIDELINES. "...a most vital source of...
URL: www.erlbaum.com/1065.htm
Translate Related pages Facts about: Lawrence Erlbaum ...

2. NIH Guide: DIET, LIFESTYLE AND CANCER IN U.S. SPECIAL POPULATIONS

DIET, LIFESTYLE AND CANCER IN U.S. SPECIAL POPULATIONS Release Date: February 23, 1998 PA NUMBER: PA-98-028 P.T. National Cancer Institute PURPOSE...
URL: www.nih.gov/grants/guide/pa-files/PA-98-028.html
Translate More pages from this site   Related pages Facts about: National Institut...

3. National Cancer Institute
Other NCI Sites: Plans & Priorities for Cancer Research. CancerNet. cancerTrials. ----- Office of the Director. Div. of Basic Sciences. Div. of...
URL: www.nci.nih.gov/
Translate More pages from this site   Related pages Facts about: National Institut...

Searching Alta Vista for "Cancer AND Center AND NOT research"
RESULTS:
1. Reading Room Index to the Comic Art Collection
Reading Room Index to the Comic Art Collection, Special Collections Division, Michigan State University Libraries: "Smocks" to "Smythe" Back to the...
URL: www.lib.msu.edu/comics/rri/srri/smo.htm
Translate   Related pages Facts about: Michigan State Un...

2. Support Groups
Jul. Aug. Sep. S. M. T. W. T. F. S. 1. 2. 3. 4. 5. 6. 7. 8. 9. 10. 11. 12. 13. 14. 15. 16. 17. 18. 19. 20. 21. 22. 23. 24. 25. 26. 27. 28. 29. 30. 31...
URL: link.chicagotribune.com/CP/calendar/1,18...-1-2000,00.html
Translate   Related pages Facts about: Tribune Tv Log

3. Special Events
Special Events. OUTREACH SKILLS TRAINING AND
INFORMATION EXCHANGE. Please call (212) 719-2943,
ext. 321. My Mother's Breast. Come and spend an...
URL: www.sharecancersupport.org/99q4/special.html
Translate   Related pages Facts about: Share

All Terms Search

Most search services support use of the Boolean "AND"
operator through one or all of the following methods:
- Implied (using an operator is unnecessary)
- Menus (for example, pull-down or radio buttons)
- A special symbol used as an operator (e.g., a plus sign
  "+")
- By literally typing "and" in the search statement as an
  operator

When the use of "+" is required by a service, all terms need to
be preceded by the symbol. As an example, a correctly formed
statement to return all pages containing both cancer and women
would appear as +cancer +women. One that includes the
symbol before only one word (i.e., +cancer women) implies the
presence of cancer with or without women.

The Boolean "AND" narrows a search by retrieving only
documents that contain every one of the keywords you enter.
The more keywords you add to the search statement, the
narrower your search becomes.

Example: truth AND justice
Example: truth AND justice AND ethics AND congress

Any Terms Search

Just like using the Boolean "AND," "OR" is supported by numerous methods.

- Implied
- Menus
- By typing "or" in the statement

When searching for any one or another word or both, it is best to qualify a search statement with parentheses and another Boolean operator. This surrounding of search elements with parentheses is known as <u>nesting</u>. Nesting is an effective way to combine several search statements into one search statement. Use parentheses to separate keywords when you are using more than one operator and three or more keywords.

Example: (scotch OR bourbon) AND NOT (beer OR wine)

For best results, always enclose OR statements in parentheses. AND operators should not be used inside parentheses.

Another example would be in constructing a statement that requires depression and either Prozac or Wellbutrin would appear as (Prozac or Wellbutrin) +depression. The same statement could also be entered correctly as (Prozac or Wellbutrin) and depression.

The Boolean "OR" expands your search by retrieving documents in which either or both keywords appear. Since the OR operator is usually used for keywords that are similar or synonymous, the more keywords you enter, the more documents will result from the search.

Example: (college OR university)
Example: (college OR university OR campus OR institution)

Excluding Terms

To exclude terms, a search service usually employs:
- Menus
- Literal inclusion
- By typing a symbol, (e.g. a minus "-" sign)

There is no implied "not," so the user must take some action to exclude a term from a search statement.

The symbol indicating exclusion must precede the word or else the search service will consider the presence of the term as optional or mandatory. Of course, this depends on how the engine interprets the absence of an operator.

A proper example of a search statement employing the minus sign to include the terms "laser" and "cornea" but not "retina" would be entered as "+laser +cornea -retina." Another way of constructing this statement is "(laser and cornea) and not retina." Even one more way of entering the preceding statement is "(laser and cornea) and not retina."

The Boolean "NOT" or "AND NOT" limits the search by retrieving only your first keyword but not the second, regardless of whether or not the first word appears in that document, too.

Example: bulimia AND NOT anorexia

Since individual search services have their own requirements for specifying exclusion, it is recommended that users carefully observe them.

The next series of pages will provide you with a brief glimpse of some Yahoo! subject directory pages. The example subject used is "market new drug".

If you're connected to the Internet, open your browser in another window by clicking www.yahoo.com

The Yahoo Directory:

To search Yahoo, type a word (or several words) into the query box on any Yahoo! page, and then hit the "Search" button (or the "Enter" key on your keyboard). Yahoo! Search will then look for any matches with your query in the Yahoo! directory.

If you aren't looking for a specific web site, Yahoo allows you to choose search terms based on the general subject about which you're inquiring. Yahoo! is best used to find web sites organized by subject. Search for Yahoo! categories instead of individual web sites. This will give you more results in categories.

Attaching plus (+) or minus (-) operators will either require or prohibit words from appearing in the search results.

Plus (+) Attaching a + to a word requires that the word be found in all of the search results. Example: drug vs. market+new+drug

Minus (-) Attaching a - in front of a word requires that the word not be found in any of the search results. Example: market+new+drug-homeopathic

Phrase Matching (" ") Use quotes around a set of words to only

find results that match the words in that exact sequence.
Example: sales force to "market new drug"

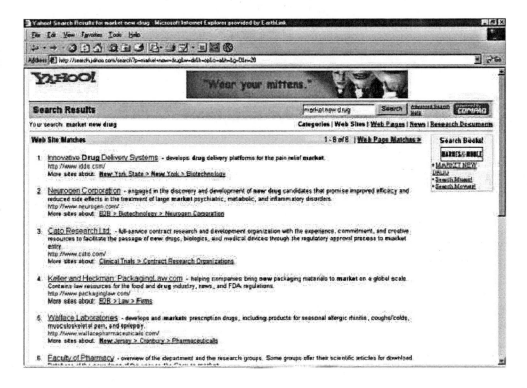

Phrase Searching

Almost every search service will return a list of documents
where two or more words appear in exact order. And, almost
every service uses quotation marks to surround the phrase as
the way to implement this feature (e.g., "Alternative
medicine").

A number of services also allow a user to phrase-search by
choosing a menu item on the same page that the user enters the
search statement.

Next we'll take a look at the HotBot search engine and perform phase searches for "market new drug (using quotation marks) and market new drug (from the menu)].

If you're connected to the Internet, open your browser in another window by clicking www.hotbot.com

HotBot results for "market new drug" (using quotation marks)
WEB RESULTS Top 10 Matches   next >>
1. The Medical Letter Home Page
The Medical Letter on Drugs and Therapeutics is an independent, peer-reviewed, non-profit publication that offers unbiased critical evaluations of drugs--with special emphasis on
http://www.medletter.com/
See results from this site only.

2. GIM Global Internet Marketing News - Newsletter
Global Internet Marketing News newsletter, internet full service provider, web development web site hosting, web site promotion, web design, search engine placement software, merchant
http://linz1.net/GIM.html
See results from this site only.

3. MLM magazine - an unbiased look at network marketing
Network Marketing and MLM Tools, Training, and Information - your online resource. Free fax-on demand. Free autoresponders. Low cost mlm leads, free MLM classified ads
http://www.networkmarketingnews.com/
See results from this site only.

Proximity Searches

Phrase searching has a variation that allows a user to locate documents where two or more words appear, but with a certain number of other terms or characters in between. The standard operator for proximity searching is "NEAR." The semantics varies among the services that offer the feature.

For example, a search statement is constructed as follows: "California near HMO." AltaVista returns documents where a maximum of ten words appears between California and HMO. Another engine, Lycos, defaults to twenty-five words.

Lycos also gives extra and extensive proximity features. The previous search statement could also be varied as follows: California far HMO (greater than twenty-five words between), California adj HMO (no words between and any order), California before HMO (any number of words between and exact order).

In addition, Lycos lets a user specify the number and order of intervening words. By preceding the operator with the letter O, order can be specified. To designate the maximum number of intervening words, append a forward slash (/) then a number. Hence, a Lycos search statement to result in all documents where California appears before HMO and with no more than five intervening words would be entered as California Onear/5 HMO.

Using Wildcards

Almost all services support the wildcard (also called stem or truncation) feature. Wildcards are handy symbols that stand in for something else. In a search word, wildcards mean "look for any word that contains these letters and (where the wildcard symbol is) any other letters. Hence, "do*" will search for "do" and "doe" and "do8" and "doings".

Wildcards are implied in some search engines, so you don't even have to enter a symbol. Every word is assumed to end with a one. Therefore, searching on "flow" will automatically dig up "flowers" and "flowbee" and any number of other words. Although this may help you retrieve items closely related to your term, it also bogs you down with lots of irrelevant results. If you have too many of these extraneous retrievals, revise the search by putting your search term inside quotation marks. Usually, this will get rid of the assumed wildcard.

Short List of Boolean Operators

Boolean operators add power to Internet searches. Use them often in order to your complex search phrases tight. Although you should check the advanced features when using individual engines and directories, here is a short list of operators that many services will recognize.
- AND is the same as & is the same as +
- OR is the same as |
- NOT is the same as ! is the same as -
- NEAR is the same as ~
- ( ) is the same as " "

Field Searching

Since Web pages contain discreet components that become searchable fields for those search services that choose to implement them in that manner. There are four components commonly used for field searching:
- Title

- URL (uniform resource locator)
- Body
- Link

Title (in search)

The document title is actually an HTML (hypertext markup language) tag and a subset of the document header. It appears on the title bar of the browser displaying the document. At the uppermost part of an application's display, the bar typically includes the name of the browser and the title of the opened document.

A title can also appear on the same page as the body, as long as the content author chooses to place it there. Most Web browsers can view the source HTML tag that contains the title. Yahoo! and AltaVista support title searching with the title: prefix (e.g., title: "Hodgkins disease treatments"). Another service, HotBot, utilizes menus.

For example, putting title: "Marketing" tells the engine that you only want pages that have "Marketing" in the title, not pages that don't have the word at all or that have it in the text, links, or other areas.

Uniform Resource Locator

The elements that make up the uniform resource locator (URL), or page address, are also used for field searching. The URL contains an address, a directory path, and a file name.

For example:

http://www.cancernet.nci.nih.gov/clinpdq.html. Here, the address (cancernet.nci.nih.gov), directory path (clinpdq), and file name (therapy.html) are separated by forward slashes (/).

To do a URL search, you typically prefix a search statement with a keyword, (e.g., url:nci.nih.gov and ti:colon). This example entered in AltaVista results in all documents from the National Cancer Institute containing the word colon in the title.

A field-supporting search engine will know that when the search line contains: "url: ebook," it should only find pages that have the word "ebook" somewhere in their URLs.

Both "http://www.ebook.com" and "http://www.example.com/ebook.html" would be retrieved, but a page from "http://www.anotherexample.com" that was all about ebooks would not, because text mention wouldn't qualify.

Body or Text

Usually, it isn't necessary to qualify that a search statement includes a Web document's body, because almost all search services default to the document text or title. Some services (e.g., Lycos) offer advanced search options using menus that specify the entire document, and these will perform a full-text search. This kind of search should be avoided, unless searching for a rare topic, because it's more costly in terms of computer resources and relevancy.

At times you may find that too many of your search engine results feel hollow, because the terms you sought are only in the title or metatags but not in the actual words on the page. This would be a good reason to try using a Text Field in your search.

An engine that supports fields would interpret this line: text: "depression drugs" to find only pages that had the phrase "depression drugs" in their text, not merely in the title or buried in the HTML code.

Citation Searching

AltaVista and HotBot offer a feature that lets you collect a list of documents that link to or cite a specified URL. Link searches can be useful for measuring the value of a Web site. Webmasters use link searching as an important tool for evaluating the merit of their content by studying who points to their pages.

Tips

Sometimes, the most difficult part of the search process is deciding where to begin. There are so many competing search services and techniques that one must learn the best ways utilize the numerous engines, directories, or metasearch engines.

-Try More Than One Search Service

Since no Internet search service exhaustively indexes the Internet, you should always use several of the largest services to perform a comprehensive search. (AltaVista, HotBot, etc.).

A site called Search IQ (www.searchiq.com) reviews search engines and sites. It shows rankings of engines, with "IQ" scores summarizing the results of the in-depth analysis and recommendations for which tool to use when.

-Read Search Service Documentation

Every search service provides online documentation that covers all of its features. Since there is no industry standard, users must realize that the syntax for one service may not be the same as for another.

-Make Use of Boolean and Field Searches

Natural language often returns relevant pages, but Boolean searching is necessary for comprehensive results.

-Be Cautious in Using Metasearch Engines

Metasearch gateways save time by repeating the same search across multiple services, but they have limitations. The common denominator sometimes used by metasearch services to work across multiple indexes may convert Boolean or field statements to natural language. Also, some search services are inaccessible to metasearch gateways. For example, few are able to reach HotBot, and none can search Northern Light.

EVALUATING INTERNET SITES

The evaluation of currency, accuracy, and authority of health care information in particular is a great concern in using the Internet as a reference service. Anybody with a computer can function simultaneously as the author, editor, and publisher of Web information. And they can do it anonymously, if they so desire!

One of the most critical aspects of health care information is accuracy, yet the Internet is fraught with published claims that are unsubstantiated and fraudulent.

A number of groups have emerged to deal with this issue of quality. The Health On the Net (HON) Foundation, a Swiss-based organization, has produced and revised the HONCode of Conduct for Medical and Health Web Sites. Sites that choose to voluntarily comply with the HONCode can display an identifying symbol.

Dedicated to promoting quality health care information on the Internet, (HON) is a nonprofit international organization. It attempts to help realize the Internet's potential as medical information resource with high merit. Many good sites do not display the HON icon, even though displaying it testifies to a site's quality. HON's full principles can be seen on the HON Web site (www.hon.ch).

Another entity, called The Health Information Technology Institute of Mitrctek Systems, Incorporated, was instrumental in creating "White Paper: Criteria for Assessing the Quality of Health Information on the Internet." A group including medical publishers, pharmaceutical companies, patient advocates, medical Internet developers, etc. and the Internet Healthcare Coalition sponsored a conference in 1998 called "Quality Healthcare Information on the 'Net '98: Delivering on the Promise."

If sites have been rated by an organization such as Physician's Choice (www.mdchoice.com/instr.htm) they can be considered to be of high quality.
These raters offer some degree of comfort, even though instruments and criteria used to rate health information have recently been shown to be inconsistent and uneven.

Practical Methods for Evaluating Web Resources

1. Check the URL name. Note what type of domain it comes from (educational, non-profit, commercial, etc.). Make sure that the domain is appropriate for the material.

- Government sites: look for .gov, .mil, .us, or other country code
- Educational sites: look for .edu or another country code
- Non-profit organizations: look for .org or some other country code

Note who "published" the page. The publisher is generally the agency or person operating the server computer from which the document is issued. The server is usually named in first portion of the URL (between http:// and the first /).

Make sure it isn't just somebody's personal page. When you read the URL carefully, you may find that the server is a commercial Internet service provider or other web page hosting company (like aol.com or geocities.com). Look for a personal name (e.g., *kjohnson* or *beckman*) following a tilde (~) or the word "users" or "people."

2. Check to see who wrote the page. Make sure that the person or authoring institution is a qualified authority.
- Look for a name and e-mail address at the bottom of the page, or in a section called "About us" or "Contact us" (or something similar). Usually this isn't the same person as the "webmaster" or page designer (except in personal pages). The webmaster is a technician or may have been hired to put the content on the web.
- Check to see that the author's credentials are provided, to make sure that this person could actually be a reliable authority on the subject. Scan the site pages (top, bottom,

side bars, etc.) for a link to an "About us" or "Biography" section, a "Philosophy," etc.

- If you can't find such a section, truncate elements of the URL to see what you can learn. In the top Location Box, delete the end characters of the URL stopping just before each / (leave the slash). To see if you can find out more about the author or the origins/nature of the site providing the page, press enter.
- Continue this, one slash (/) at a time, until you reach the first part, the domain name portion, which is the page's "publisher" (see next section).
- It is often possible to find out who owns the domain name via provided names, phone, and fax numbers.

3. Check how current, timely or dated the page is. Note when the pages were updated last. See if you can tell how much was updated. This information is usually at the bottom of the bottom of the page. Since individual pages may be updated at different times; look at more than one.

Look at the browser's "Page Info" (right click in the page, or look under View | Page Info). If this is out of date, be suspicious of a stale page. You should still be suspicious if it is current: sometimes Page Info is changed, but nothing else.

Review the site's other pages. Follow the procedure detailed above to truncate back the URL and view "parent" or related pages. Not all pages are updated at the same time. Make sure that the date is appropriate for the content.

Also, be sure that it isn't "stale" or "dusty" information, especially on a time-sensitive or evolving topic. Be warned that undated factual or statistical information is no better than anonymous information. It shouldn't be used.

4. Check to see that information cited is authentic. Make certain that if the page claims to be from an established newspaper, journal, organization, institution, or agency, it is a real one.

Check whether the domain name corresponds to the source. Most companies and institutions own their own names. If in doubt, check the owner of the domain name. Government sites should be .gov, .mil, or some .us, or from another country's official sites.

Check to see that it is unmodified, if it purports to be a reproduction, facsimile, or excerpt of a published piece. Someone could easily copy and tinker with the content of a page and put it back on the Web with copies of the original logo, banners, credits, and other information. Locate the original to be sure, either elsewhere on the Web or try the library's reference desk.

5. Make sure that the source of factual or attributed information is well documented. Without your being able to certify the content by the reputation of a known publisher or institution, establish the following requirement for your research: sources and claims must be substantiated by links to reliable sources or references (e.g., notes or footnotes as in a published work).

Beware: Footnoting and citing standards regarding where people obtained information (and when) are extremely loose on the Web and much less exacting that in most print publications. Make sure you can find the source and date for attributed information, or you shouldn't use it. If you can't find the source on line, a reference librarian may be able to help you locate it.

6. Make sure the page has overall integrity and reliability as a source.

Ascertain the page's purpose, i.e., why it was created. As a motive, some were created to inform and explain facts or data. Others are designed to persuade, promote or just sell. Additional objectives for Web page content are to share, disclose, rant and/or entice.

Review who else links to the page, and where this is "cited." See if you can tell what they think of the page's quality and integrity. Scan for awards (or links to an "Awards" page) from reputable directories and guides. Browse these and note what they say. Check out the award, and don't just take it at face value.

A search engine like Google or AltaVista can help you see who links to the page. Maybe a visit to some of the engine or directory sites will reveal what they say about the page in question. In Google or Alta Vista, precede the URL by the term link: with no space after the colon.

> Example: In the search box, enter:
> link:www.whitehouse.net

> In Google Advance Search put the URL in the box labeled "Find pages that link to the page."

Look for the page in a reliably annotated subject directory. Examples: Librarians' Index, Infomine, About.com (quality of annotations varies), and Scout Report.

7. Check the site's bias. Find out who sponsors the page and whether the sponsors may have a vested interest in the viewpoint presented.

- Look for links to "sponsors," "About us," "Philosophy," etc. Advertisers can also be sponsors. Try to determine if the points of view could be constrained or bent to keep or attract advertisers.

- Scan for links to other viewpoints, which may be balanced or annotated. Note if there is anything that's not said that could be said. Also note whether or not this would be said if all points of view were represented. Try to think of alternative viewpoints, and ask if they are represented or linked to.

- Look for your own bias to make sure that you are being completely fair. Be certain that you are totally objective and maybe not too harsh. Require the same degree of "proof" that you would demand from a print publication.
- Note whether the site is good for some things and not for others. Make sure that your hopes do not bias your interpretation.

8. Note whether the page or site has an ironic, satirical, or a spoof-like tone. Some pages that appear to be factual are actually meant to be humorous, parodied, exaggerated, or overblown arguments for the sake of entertaining. Look out for outrageous photographs or juxtaposition of unlikely images.

9. Contact the author or publisher if you have questions or reservations.
- E-mail the author or publisher to request additional background.
- Consult a print publication in the Library, if necessary.
- Seek advice at a library reference desk or speak with an instructor, if you're enrolled in a class.

10. If you need to get to the source, the following techniques will sometimes allow you to investigate domain name owners. Read the domain name for a clue to the type of page (with skepticism).

- Look up the domain registry page at the appropriate registry agency:
- For .com, .edu, .net, .org :
  http://www.networksolutions.com/cgi-bin/whois/whois
- For .gov (U.S. government) : http://www.nic.gov/cgi-bin/whois
- For .mil (U.S. military) : http://www.nic.mil/cgi-bin/whois
- For Asian-Pacific : http://www.apnic.net/apnic-bin/whois.pl
- For European : http://www.ripe.net/cgi-bin/whois
- For the rest of the world:
  http://www.uninett.no/navn/domreg.html

Review the credentials of the authors and editors, since a medical doctor (MD), doctor of chiropractic (DC), and doctor of osteopathy (DO) will each have his or her own biases.

Good sites also identify areas that have been newly updated and have a minimum of obsolete links.

When a site with information aimed at patients is one of quality, it will undoubtedly display a statement that the information is not intended as a replacement for the advice of a professional physician and that the patient should discuss any concerns with his or her medical practitioner, especially prior to beginning or changing any treatments or therapies.

SELECTED SEARCH SERVICES

Answer Services

When you want to retrieve and/or browse health information, you have the option of using several types of resources. In addition to engines, directories and mega sites, you can also use answer services, such as Allexperts, AskJeeves, and LookSmart.

Allexperts (www.allexperts.com)

This site is supplied by volunteers with expertise in 1,500 topic areas as diverse as: car repair, health, travel, and music. Many physicians and health professionals answer questions posed to the site. Yet some of the volunteers provide advice without professional credentials. These may base their answers on personal experience and anecdotes.

Ask Jeeves (www.askjeeves.com) or (www.ask.com)

This service interprets and processes questions stated in plain English (natural language searching). If Jeeves can't understand a question, it requests that you state the query differently or change the spelling.

A typical Jeeves query is *"where can I find information on prostate cancer or drugs for depression."* Jeeves attempts to match questions with "answers" within its own database, and then uses an external search engine when it fails to make a match.

Looksmart (www.looksmart.com)

LookSmart gives you a glimpse of what other users are searching, besides allowing you to perform natural language searching and to pose search questions. This service has a personal health channel that features live search editors that promise search help responses within twenty-four hours. Other categories include "Diseases/conditions," "Diet & Nutrition," "Drugs & Medicines," "Natural Therapies," and more.

ENGINES AND DIRECTORIES

Selected Engines and Directories

Currently, more than 1,500 search engines are in operation. This makes the task of learning the features or capabilities of each one difficult. To keep up with the changes in scope, or for updates on comparisons, use the resources of Search Engine Watch (www.searchenginewatch.com).

The five engines/directories below (AltaVista, FAST Search, GO/Infoseek, Google, Northern Light, and Yahoo) have variable sizes, complexities of interface, and available search options. These services are some of the most powerful search tools on the Internet.

AltaVista (www.altavista.com)

AltaVista is among the largest search engines. It possesses numerous syntax features that both novice and expert searchers find useful. Some of these are: plus and minus signs, Boolean operators, parentheses to combine multiple ideas, and field searching (title, link, uniform resource locator). "Ask AltaVista" allows natural language searching, with results derived from Ask Jeeves. The estimated size of AltaVista is 250 million pages.

FAST Search (www.alltheweb.com)

FAST Search was formerly known as All The Web. This service distinguishes itself with its sheer speed and simple search interface page. Search statements can be posed as "all the words," "any of the words," and "the exact phrase." FAST Search's estimated size is 200 million pages.

GO/Infoseek (www.go.com) or (www.infoseek.com)

GO is a portal site, which is produced jointly by Infoseek and Disney. It gives superior search engine and site directory performances, and interface customization. Included in its syntax features are the ability to use the pipe (|) to search within, plus and minus signs, quotations for searching phrases, and field searching (title, link uniform resource locator, site). GO's estimated size is 75 million pages.

Google (www.google.com)

Google is different from other search engines in that it uses link popularity to rank Web sites. For example, if lots of site developers link to a specific health resource, this could be interpreted as a vote of confidence for the site's unique characteristics or usefulness. The interface at Google is among the simplest and easiest to use. Google's estimated size is 85 million pages.

Northern Light (www.northernlight.com)

Northern Light is one of the largest Web indexes. It supports natural language searching, but use of specific keywords is more important than phrasing questions. This service searches both the Web and its own fee-based special collection. Northern Light's special collection documents are available to free searching, yet you have to pay per document to view them.

Among this resource's interesting features are special limits (dates, subjects, or types of sites), field searching (title, uniform resource locator, and text within a site), and sorting by relevance and/or date. Northern Light's estimated size is 189 million pages.

Yahoo (www.yahoo.com)

Yahoo is a sponsored directory, and is tiny in comparison to other search services. But its easy-to-use and well-organized approach to information more than compensates for any lack of size. The resource's small catalog is supplemented with results by the Inktomi search engine (www.inktomi.com). Yahoo offers a health channel, which includes various health sections, including one for women's health. Yahoo's estimated size is 1.2 million pages.

Medical Search Engines

The above search services are quite able to locate and retrieve health-related sites. Yet, search engines specific to medicine and health allow for better search precision, and they cut down on extraneous and irrelevant results.

Example: a simple search on mumps, using a general search engine, might yield unrelated hits about the computer programming language, MUMPS.

Achoo Healthcare Online (www.achoo.com/main.asp)

Achoo is a powerful medical search engine developed and maintained in Canada. Among its features are "Site of the Week," "Reference Sources" (journals, databases, directories, statistics), "Healthcare News," Famous Quotes," and voting polls.

CiteLine.com (www.citeline.com)

Sponsored by Caredata.com, a health care market intelligence firm, this site is geared to professionals and serious consumers. Some of its features include limiting searches to "Disease & Treatment," "News & Journal "Organizations," and "Research & Trials." The search engine is case sensitive.

Medical World Search
(www.enigma.co.nz/mws/mws_source.htm)

Medical World Search uses more than 500,000 medical terms from the National Library Medicine's Unified Medical Language System to query other search engines and to deliver focused results. Special features require a one-time user registration. One such feature is the option to obtain recalls of your last queries or last 10 sites visited.

MedExplorer (www.medexplorer.com)

Geared toward the health professional, MedExplorer contains internal search capabilities, along with "Health-Exam" (drug database, MEDLINE, body mass index calculator, etc.), discussion forums and chat, more than 250 searchable health newsgroups, "Palm Health Zone (hand held computing applications)," "Conferences," and more. MedExplorer allows you to search categories ranging from alternative medicine to vision, plus daily health tips. A feature called "Ask Doc" from InteliHealth (www.intelihealth.com) is also featured on Discovery Health (www.discoveryhealth.com).

MedHunt (www.hon.ch/MedHunt)

MedHunt was developed by the Swiss-based Health on the Net (HON) Foundation. There are two parts to its database: HONored sites that have been visited and annotated by humans, and the auto-indexed database compiled by an electronic spider. MedHunt offers the ability to search all the words, any of the words, and adjacent words. It also allows you to limit retrieval display to all sites, HONored sites, hospitals, support, events, and by geographical region.

Name & Web Address	Database	Boolean	Other Search Options
AltaVista **www.altavista.com**	Full text of Web pages (340M+) Ask Jeeves question answers (7M+) Discussion group postings (RemarQ) RealNames corporate, product finder.	+ to require. - to remove. Phrase (if detected) then Fuzzy OR - default. Advanced Search only: AND, OR, AND NOT, NEAR, Nesting ( ); Sort by: terms here activate results ranking.	Quotes for phrase. * to truncate. Case-sensitive, Can use "natural" language. Limit by date, language. Fields: domain: host: image: title: url: link: like: anchor: applet:
Google **www.google.com**	Full text of Web pages (650M, + 652M partially indexed URLs)	AND - default. + only to include stop words or to require specific	Quotes for phrase. Fields: link: site: Uncle Sam

	Caches indexed pages - great for finding 404s	domain in URL or on page (e.g., +edu). - to remove.	(.gov & .mil) Can search within subject directory categories. 26 languages.
Hotbot **www.hot bot.com**	Full text of Web pages (500M+) Partner Databases: Cars (Autoweb), Jobs (CareerBuilder), Stocks (Stockpoint), News (30 days worth), E-mail & White Pages (BigYellow), Yellow Pages (At Hand)	+ to require. - to remove. AND - default (all of these words); OR (any of these words); NOT: and PHRASE (can also use quotes) Select Boolean and can nest ( ).	Quotes for phrase. * to truncate. Case-sensitive. From drop-down box: search by title, person, link, or Boolean. Can limit by language, date, location, page depth. Fields: title: domain: feature:, etc.
Yahoo **www.yah oo.com**	Submitted Web pages (2M+) Topic & region specific Yahoos - Kids (Yahooligans), Japan, SF Bay, etc.	+ to require. - to remove. AND (default), OR (options only)	Quotes for phrase. * to truncate. Fields: t:title; u:URL

Some search engines form strategic partnerships to combine power and to give users better services. To achieve more relevant results or to supplement their own search engine or directory, major search engines make use of different technologies.

One of the reasons that some engines partner with other sites is to become hybrid: both a search engine and a directory. This hybrid capacity is shared by all of the major search engines. Some buy directory or database services from the already existing engines, while others compile their own.

The most popular directory on the web is Yahoo!, which buys Google's results for their "Web Pages" section. For more complete results, other search engines may also choose to use each other's services. Inktomi and DirectHit are services that are used not only to complete results, but to make them more accurate by overlaying various technologies.

The table below describes some of the search engine partnerships. Knowing this information will allow you to better understand how each search engine works so that you can make effective submissions. As an example, you should submit AOL Search queries to Inktomi and Open Directory Project, instead of AOL.

Search engine partnerships

Search Engine	AOL Search	Altavista Search Engine	Go/ Infoseek Directory	Google Search Engine	Hotbot Search Engine	iWon Search Engine
Uses its own engine or index	No	Yes	Yes	Yes	No	No

Inktomi*	Yes	No	No	No	Yes	Yes
Direct Hit **	No	No	Yes, Infoseek	No	Yes	Yes
Real Names ***	No	Yes, appears before search results	Yes	Yes	No	Yes
New! GoTo.com	Yes, first 3 results	Yes, top 5 results.	No	No	Yes, results	No
Powered by:	Open Directory	LookSmart Directory, Ask Jeeves	No	Open Directory	Open Directory	LookSmart
Provides search results for other search engines	No	No	No	Yes, Yahoo	No	No

Review Question: Which of the following is true of answer services?

A. Search queries must use Boolean operators.

B. Questions stated in plain English are interpreted and processed.

C. Proximity locators are necessary for good results.

Answer: B is correct; e.g., "How do I find distributors and buyers of eye laser equipment?"

SEARCH TROUBLESHOOTING

- If the search returns far too many documents:

  You probably typed only one (and common) term. Find some synonyms or try adding at least two more specific terms to your string.

- If the search returns too few documents:

  Either your search statement is too narrow, or you're probably searching in the wrong place. It's possible that you didn't configure your search correctly. It's also possible that the information you seek may not be on the Web. Try deleting some of your search terms. Attempt the search on another engine, directory, people search, or specialty resource. Request help.

- If the search returns a "404 -- file not found" message:

  This notification means that the file you're looking for has been moved, removed, or renamed. Return to the search engine and perform a phrase search or a field search on the title. Experiment with shortening the URL to see if the file might still be on the same server.

- If the search returns a "server does not have a DNS entry" message:

  This notification means that your browser can't locate the server (i.e. the computer that hosts the web page). The network could be busy or the server may have been removed or taken down for maintenance. Review your spelling and make another search attempt later.

- If your search returns a "server error" or "server is busy" message:

  The server you're trying to contact may be offline, may have crashed, or may be very busy. Make another search attempt later. (If you need more information on error codes, search for CNET's: Internet Errors Explained: What Went Wrong? What Can I Do? by Shirley Malcolm.)

- If you can't find the home page for a well-known product or organization:

Try to guess by experimenting with different top-level domain names, if necessary. Lots of organizations have their name, brief name, or acronym as their URL.

Example: www.iomega.com; www.redcross.org (Sometimes this doesn't work).

Example: You won't find the American Medical Association this way. The "ama" acronym was snagged first by the American Marketing Association. In the same way, Delta Financial Corporation beat out Delta Airlines. (But this technique is good for a first try.)

Try a URL search, using the name, brief name, or acronym. One final method: if your browser is a recent Netscape upgrade, type in the word or phrase with nothing else and, if Netscape can match it, it will take you to the site automatically.

How to Search for Diseases

There is no "best way" to search the Internet for disease information. Information abounds for high profile and prevalent diseases (e.g., AIDS, asthma, cancer, diabetes, etc.), which generate extensive interest in the general public. These diseases can have considerable research funding, along with having their own associations, foundations, or even institutes.

Other, less known diseases may be more difficult to find on the Web. Rare diseases, those which may be perceived as not affecting the general population, and those which don't generate serious research dollars, are not as easy to locate. Other types of disease not easily found include those that don't fit well into one disease category and emerging diseases and therapies. The methods of searching must be altered according to the specific disease.

One of the ways to begin a search for information about a disease is to look at known sites of quality on the subject. Next, visit general medical sites that specialize in organizing and providing information. Diseases like cancer have substantial Web representation.

As an example, consider how one might search for information about cancer. Using selected medical sites will demonstrate universal concepts and methods for searching the Web. Cancer is a common disease, so it isn't surprising to find a number of quality sites on the Web devoted entirely to this affliction. Two representative sites are: Oncolink (www.oncolink.upenn.edu) and CancerNet (www.cancernet.nci.nih.gov).
Oncolink gives you the capacity to find information from several perspectives. The Oncolink home page gives a choice of selections. These range from "Disease Oriented Menus,"

"Medical Specialty Oriented Menus," and "Clinical Trials," to "Psychosocial Support and Personal Experiences." "Search Oncolink" is another feature with a link on the home page.

The University of Pennsylvania maintains the site. Links from the home page take you to "About Oncolink" and "Editorial Board" which post where information comes from.

There is a vast range of disease-related material on the Internet. It ranges from practitioner-oriented clinical information to patient/consumer resources. Some sites, e.g. NOAH (www.noah.cuny.edu), are designed primarily for consumers; whereas, some are specifically for physicians, e.g., CliniWeb (www.ohsu.edu/cliniweb).

Sites like CancerNet (www.cancernet.nci.nih.gov) may feature a range of information, with page links that arbitrarily separate those resources that are practitioner oriented from the consumers'.

Disease information on the Web is free most of the time, and it's available to all with access. Commercial vendors often do not provide free information to the public or to libraries, though. Also, a number of sites require that you register as a user, even if the resources are offered without a fee.

To find diverse resources under a single roof, look to organizations, associations, foundations, institutions, societies, agencies, and clearinghouses. These groups have a diverse set of missions, and most of the quality sites include a mission statement somewhere among their pages. Included in this statement is description of the audience to which they seek to appeal. Organizations can serve consumers or clinicians, and some partition their services with separate links for each contingent group.

Some of the consumer-oriented cancer sites include:

The American Cancer Society (www.cancer.org)

This organization gives information about cancer prevention, treatment, and survivorship.

The National Institutes of Health (NIH) (www.nih.gov)

NIH is one of the world's premiere biomedical research centers. It is composed of a group of twenty-four smaller institutes, including the National Cancer Institute (www.nci.nih.gov).

The Centers for Disease Control and Prevention (CDC) (www.cdc.gov).

CDC is an agency of the Department of Health and Human Services. Its stated mission is to promote "health and quality of life by preventing and controlling disease, injury, and disability. Disease information is organized alphabetically under the link called "Health Information." This is a high-quality site.

Medical gateway sites can be some of the best locations for beginning a disease information search. This is primarily because of their duty to offer a range of resources-database searching. But they're also helpful in that they provide general information for the consumer and researcher-all from within one site.

Theory Summary

The Internet is a vast garden of resources on almost every subject imaginable and for every walk in life. The preceding material will help you search the Internet for information, specifically of a medical nature. The techniques and services described are applicable to finding information on any topic.

Exercise: Marketing a New Depression Drug

Benjamin Cooper is an executive at the Stellar Pharmaceutical Company, which is considering the marketing of a new depression drug. The company wants to call it "Cheeruptime," but no research has been done yet to see if anyone else is using that name.

Ben must:

1. Register the name "Cheeruptime" at the patent and trademark offices.

2. Register a Web site with the name "cheeruptime.com" before it's taken by anyone else.

3. Check on clinical trials in which to test this drug.

4. Get drug price comparisons.

5. Check out sales of antidepressants to pharmacies and hospitals.

6. Check out manage care companies' coverage of drugs and treatment procedures. Find out which treatments they cover, and whether they prefer giving drugs to therapy.

7. Perform other market research (statistical information)

8. Contract a sales force.

9. Hire an advertising firm.

Unlike Dr. Roberts' research assistant, Tanya, Ben Cooper had garnered much experience with Internet searching. And he knew many of the same tools and "tricks" that Dr. Roberts had left for Tanya's instruction.

These are the results of Ben's search:

Registration of the name "Cheeruptime" at the patent and trade mark offices

Ben searched the U.S. Patent and Trademark Office (www.uspto.gov) and found that the "Cheeruptime" name has not been registered by any other entity as of the current date.

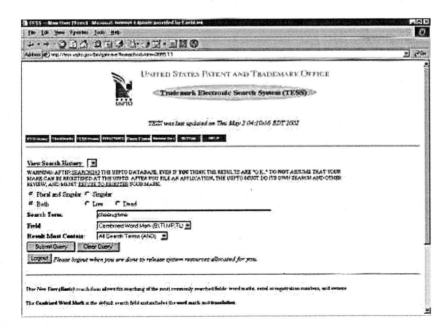

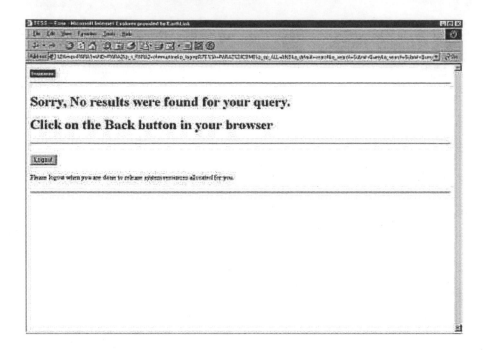

Registration of a Web site with the name "cheeruptime.com" before it's taken by anyone else.

Whois.net (www.whois.net) - provides information on who's who among the currently registered 19,826,172 com, net, and org domain names, as well as the 527,792 on hold and the 2,515,087 that have been deleted.

Clinical trials in which to test this drug

CenterWatch Clinical Trials Listing Service (www.centerwatch.com) - is a listing of clinical trials.

ClinicalTrials.gov (www.clinicaltrials.gov/ct/gui/c/b))

Search the Studies (www.clinicalstudies.info.nih.gov/)

American College of Physicians (ACP) (www.acponline.org)

Association of Health Care Policy and Research (AHCPR)
(www.ahcpr.gov)

Clinical Trials Search Builder (www.recap.com) - A service
that allows the entry of values needed to search a company's
database of Clinical Trials.

Drug price comparisons

ExactOne.com (www.exactone.com) - An engine & "bot" to
find services, jobs, books, etc. It can compare prices, shipping
schedules and costs, inventory status, etc.

WebShopper (www.webshopper.com) - features PC World
Reviews, Buyers Guides, price comparisons and unbiased
advice, all in one convenient location.

Merck-Medco (www.merckmedco.com)

Sales of antidepressant to pharmacies and hospitals
Worldwide Drugs (www.community.net/~neils/ncw.html)

International Pharmaceutical Federation
(www.pharmweb.net/pwmirror/pw9/fip/pharmweb92.html)

DrugText (www.drugtext.nf)

Medical-Net's "Hospital Select" (www.hospitalselect.com)- a
reference source of information on individual hospitals in the
United State.

AMA Physician Select, On-Line Doctor Finder (www.ama-
assn.org/aps/amahg.htm) - gives information concerning the
specialists who can treat any specific disease.

American Hospital Association (AHA) (www.aha.org)

Joint Commission on Accreditation of Health Care
Organizations (JCAHO) (www.jcaho.org)

Hospital Select (www.hospitalselect.com)

Health-Mart (www.health-mart.net)

Managed care companies' coverage of drugs and treatment
procedures-- which treatments they cover, and their preference
of giving drugs as opposed to therapy:

Health Care Financing Administration (HCFA)
(www.hcfa.gov/) - is responsible for providing information on
qualification criteria, benefits, application procedures, and
managed care services for Medicare, Medicaid, and Child
Health Insurance programs.

Kaiser Permanente (www.kaiserpermanente.org) - is the largest
not-for-profit health maintenance organization in the country
with 7.5 million members.

Group Health Cooperative of Puget Sound (www.ghc.org) - is
the nation's sixth largest not-for-profit HMO, serving over
700,000 members in the northwestern United States.

The American Association of Health Plans (AAHP)
(www.aahp.org) - This organization represents more than 1,000
HMOs and other network based plans, and serves over 100
million Americans nationwide.

The Health Insurance Association of America (HIAA) (www.hiaa.org) - is a trade association whose members are insurance companies and managed care companies.

The Blue Cross and Blue Shield Association (www.bluescares.com) - provides links to all the regional associations.

Kaiser Permanente (www.kaiserpermanente.org) - is the largest not-for-profit health maintenance organization in the country with 7.5 million members.

Group Health Cooperative of Puget Sound (www.ghc.org) - is the nation's sixth largest not-for-profit HMO, serving over 700,000 members in the northwestern United States.

The American Association of Health Plans (AAHP) (www.aahp.org) - This organization represents more than 1,000 HMOs and other network based plans, and serves over 100 million Americans nationwide.

The National Committee for Quality Assurance (NCQA) (www.ncqa.org) - is an independent, not-for-profit organization that serves as the accrediting agency for the nation's managed care plans. NCQA maintains HEDIS 3.0, the standard report card used to rate and compare managed care plans. Links to HEDIS 3.0 may be found at the NCQA web site.

The accounting firm Price Waterhouse (www.pwcglobal.com) maintains an active consulting practice in the managed care industry. Access survey and research information through their web site.

Health Economics—Places to Go (www.medecon.de/hec.htm) - supplies links to sites related to health economics, health policy, managed care, and more.

Other market research (statistical information, demographics, etc.)

Department of Health and Human Services (DHHS) (www.os.dhhs.gov)

National Center for Health Statistics (NCHS) (www.cdc.gov/nchswww/) - the premier federal government agency responsible for collecting, analyzing, and disseminating health statistics.

Social Security Agency Office of Research Evaluation and Statistics (www.ssa.gov/statistics/ores_home.html) k

State and Metropolitan Area Data Book (www.census.gov/prod/www/abs/msgen11c.html)

Medical-Net's "Hospital Select" (www.hospitalselect.com) - a reference source of information on individual hospitals in the United State.

AMA Physician Select, On-Line Doctor Finder (www.ama-assn.org/aps/amahg.htm) - gives information concerning the specialists who can treat any specific disease.

Other government sites

Federal Drug Administration (www.fda.gov)
Federal Trade Commission (www.ftc.gov/)

Sales force contracts

Ventiv Health U.S. Sales (www.company.monster.com/snydh/)
or (www.company.occ.com/snydh)
Ashfield Healthcare (www.ashfield-uk.com/)

Contract Sales Conference
(www.clinmark.com/wwwboard/board6/messages/45.html)

Advertising contract firms

(www.4advertising.com)
(www.abelson-taylor.com/html/whoweare/01_who.html)
(www.adage.com/international/)
(www.adassoc.org.uk/)
(www.adweek.com/)
(www.agencyfinder.com)
(www.airon.it)

Online business (e-commerce) services

(www.earthlink.net)
(www.aol.com)
(www.garage.com)
(www.directmarketing-online.com)

End:

Benjamin Cooper was very successful with his research for
"Cheeruptime." Over the next few years, the Stellar
Pharmaceutical Company dominated the depression drug
market, making millions of dollars in orders.

Ben looked back with pride on his ability to search the Web for information. As he and his family enjoyed a bonus vacation, Ben sipped from his soft drink with ice, while basking on a Caribbean beach.

The Cancer Center Research

A few days later, Tanya sat alone in the doctor's office and turned the last page of his textbook on medical Internet searching.

"Where on earth do I start?!" she thought out loud.

After connecting to the ISP and opening her browser, Tanya stared blankly at the screen.

"Well, according to the book, there's no one single way to begin a search. And since the search method needs to change depending upon what's being searched for, maybe I should start with a directory, like Yahoo!"

But then she shook her head. "No, I should try one of the search engines, since Yahoo! will only give me results based on who paid to be in their databases."

Finally she made a decision. "First I'll use a metasearch service that will hit multiple engines and some directories too. Then, I'll click to find relevant sites, and navigate from their related links to other target sites."

Tanya sat up, bright-eyed and excited. She entered multiple search queries in Copernic (a free metasearch download). Then she tried some of the other metasearch gateways, as well as individual engines and directories, including those specific to medicine.

Experimenting with the use of the Boolean operators AND (+), AND NOT (-), and OR, Tanya next began to pinpoint the sites she needed. She also employed proximity locators, such as NEAR, ADJ, and numerical values, as the individual search services allowed.

Eventually, she had to apply the nesting technique of using parentheses to combine several search statements into one search statement. Tanya found it very useful to separate keywords with these parentheses when she found herself working with more than one operator and three or more keywords.

The task so daunted Tanya that she quickly found herself overwhelmed with the sheer volume of sites retrieved. Some of them were useful, but many were irrelevant. At one point, she became so frustrated, that she was about to call Dr. Roberts and ask him to hire someone else. But something inside her said, "No! You've got to walk through the process first. Then, if you don't find enough useful sites, you can give up."

Tanya heeded her inner voice. She diligently applied the search course information that Dr. Robert had left with her, particularly his list of Internet Search Tools. And to her amazement, she found them more than adequate in helping her to locate information on any topic-- or subtopic... and in any category-- or sub category!

Empowered with her new mastery of Internet searches, Tanya retrieved the following results for her report on how to open a cancer center in conjunction with Dr. Roberts' local hospital.

Hospital construction companies

- Peck Jones (www.peckjones.com) - (Southern California) Provides general construction, program management, construction management, and engineering consulting: commercial, industrial and institutional buildings.
- AC Martin Partners
- Altoon+Porter Architechs - portfolio includes retail, office, residential, hotel, multi-use, historic preservation, adaptive re-use, institutional, and entertainment facilities.
- Archigraph - experienced in 3D architectural modelling and rendering.
- Architecture International
- Built By Design, Inc. - Los Angeles and Orange County architect and contractor serving design, build, and remodel needs.
- Burning Box
- Central Office of Architecture - engaging in residential and commercial projects.
- Clive Wilkinson Architects - focusing on workplace design, uban design, office buildings, furniture, residences, and boutiques.

And as Tanya continued to search, she found hundreds of companies!

Starting a business:

Theme Hospital (www.eudoxus.demon.co.uk/) - a service specializing in hospital design and construction. They also give consultation on such subjects as general good practice, creative staff management, and patient care, as well as training and research.

American Academy of Medical Practice Analysts - provide instruction and consultation designed to enhance the ability of medical practices to function at peak efficiency levels (via staffing, startup and operating analyses, sales, marketing, and advertising).

Garage.com (www.garage.com) provides startup companies with resources on professional services (e.g., acccounting & tax, banking, consulting, insurance, legal, recruiting and executive search).

Staffing (oncologists, nurses, medical assistants, etc.)

American Association of Orthopaedic Surgeons (www.aaos.org)
MedCareers (www.medcareers.com)
AMA Physician Select (www.ama-assn.org)
American Board of Medical Specialties (ABMS) (www.abms.org)
DocFinder (www.docfinder.org)
Oncology.com (www.oncology.com)
(www.es-chamber.com/members.html) - lists temporary and permanent employment agency sites (e.g., appleone.com, volt.com, etc.)
 Ijive.com (www.ijive.com)

Community demographics and other statistics

Department of Health and Human Services (DHHS) (www.os.dhhs.gov)
National Center for Health Statistics (NCHS) (www.cdc.gov/nchswww/)) - the premier federal government agency responsible for collecting, analyzing, and disseminating health statistics.

Social Security Agency Office of Research Evaluation and
Statistics
(www.ssa.gov/statistics/ores_home.html)
State and Metropolitan Area Data Book
(www.census.gov/prod/www/abs/msgen11c.htm.
CancerNet (www.cancernet.nci.nih.gov)
The Centers for Disease Control and Prevention (CDC)
(www.cdc.gov)
Medical-Net's "Hospital Select" (www.hospitalselelect.com) a
reference source of information on individual hospitals in the
United States.

Competition

Cancer Treatment Centers of America
(www.cancercenter.com/home/)
Cedars Sinai Medical Center
(www.csmc.edu/commons/search/sitesearch.htm)
Cedar Sinai Medical Center Cancer Group -
(mailto:cancer.web@cshs.org)
Medical-Net's "Hospital Select" (www.hospitalselect.com) a
reference source of information on individual hospitals in the
United State.
AMA Physician Select, On-Line Doctor Finder (www.ama-
assn.org/aps/amahg.htm) - gives information concerning the
specialists who can treat any specific disease.
American Hospital Association (AHA) (www.aha.org)
Joint Commission on Accreditation of Health Care
Organizations (JCAHO) (www.jcaho.org)

Drugs

FDA drug approvals for cancer indications
(www.fda.gov/oashi/cancer/cdrug.html)
PharmInfo.com (www.pharminfo.com)
Mediconsultinc.com (www.mediconsultinc.com)
Merck Medco (www.merck-medco.com/medco/index.jsp)
Harrison's Online (www.harrisononline.com)

Insurance

The Health Insurance Association of America (HIAA)
(www.hiaa.org) - is a trade association whose members are
insurance companies and managed care companies

The Blue Cross and Blue Shield
Association (www.bluescares.com) - provides links to all the
regional associations.

Managed care

Agency for Health Care Policy and Research (AHCPR)
(www.ahcpr.gov/) - Among other functions, this agency
provides survey information, such as the Medical Expenditure
Panel Survey on health care utilization, expenditures, and
insurance coverage for defined populations.

Health Care Financing Administration (HCFA)
(www.ahcpr.gov/ - is responsible for providing information on
qualification criteria, benefits, application procedures, and
managed care services for Medicare, Medicaid, and Child
Health Insurance programs.

Health Economics –Places to Go (www.medecon.de/hec.htm) -
supplies links to sites related to health economics, health policy,
managed care, and more.

The Health Insurance Association of America (HIAA) (www.hiaa.org) - is a trade association whose members are insurance companies and managed care companies.

The Blue Cross and Blue Shield Association (www.bluescares.com) - provides links to all the regional associations.

Kaiser Permanente (www.kaiserpermanente.org) - is the largest not-for-profit health maintenance organization in the country with 7.5 million members.

Group Health Cooperative of Puget Sound (www.ghc.org) - is the nation's sixth largest not-for-profit HMO, serving over 700,000 members in the northwestern United States.

The American Association of Health Plans (AAHP) (www.aahp.org) - This organization represents more than 1,000 HMOs and other network based plans, and serves over 100 million Americans nationwide.

The National Committee for Quality Assurance (NCQA) (www.ncqa.org) - is an independent, not-for-profit organization that serves as the accrediting agency for the nation's managed care plans. NCQA maintains HEDIS 3.0, the standard report card used to rate and compare managed care plans. Links to HEDIS 3.0 may be found at the NCQA web site.

The accounting firm Price Waterhouse (www.pwcglobal.com) maintains an active consulting practice in the managed care industry. Access survey and research information through their web site.

Organizations

American Medical Assn. (www.ama-assn.org)
The National Institutes of Health (NIH) (www.nih.gov)
American Psychological Association (www.apa.org)

Journal articles on cancer care centers

University of Texas M.D. Anderson Cancer Center: Medical
Journals Online
(www.mdacc.tmc.edu/~library/Mejoonln/MJOlinks.htm)
Journal of the American Medical Association (JAMA)
(www.ama-assn.org)

Medical equipment supplies

(www.ablerents.com/)
(www.acartequipment.superb.net/home.html)
(www.ahsinc.com/hospital.htm)
(www.boardheaven.communitech.net/buysellboard/messages/4
27.html)
(www.disc-medicalsupply.com/)
(www.hospital-supplies.health-care1.com)
(www.chemnet.com)

Equipment auctions

(www.constantauction.com)
(www.yahoo.com)
(www.lablots.com/)
(www.medbids.com)

Office supplies

(www.company.monster.com/staples/)

(www.pages.prodigy.net/selfdefense/officemax.html)
(www.accreditedmedicalsupplies.com/medical_equipment_sup
ply.shtml

Online business (e-commerce) services

(www.earthlink.net)
(www.aol.com)

This concludes Tanya's cancer center research.

She was very successful!

The Prostate Cancer Research

After locating the information on starting a hospital cancer
center, Tanya used the momentum and energy of her success to
go right into searching for the latest prostate cancer treatments.
But even though she clicked the "Diseases" and "Cancer" links
on the medical sites she'd previously found, she didn't quite
feel as if she'd gotten the absolute latest treatment procedures in
her results.

"Oh, I remember!" Tanya thought out loud. "Searching for a
disease is different than searching for how to start up a
business." She proceeded to review the Medical Internet Search
text on ways to search specifically for diseases and treatments.

"First, I'll visit cancer organization sites, both consumer and
professional. Then I'll look at some of the government sites to
find out about clinical trials and new developments. I'll also
utilize the medicine-specific search engines and directories to
see what else I can find. And there are a few of those

miscellaneous tools on Dr. Roberts' miscellaneous tool list that I haven't tried yet."

Tanya viewed and utilized those sites, then clicked to sites that accessed MEDLINE. Next, she queried medical metasearch engines and surfed to virtually every site mentioned in the text materials that Dr. Roberts had given her.

Smiling with pride, Tanya was on a roll.

And her search retrieved the following results:

The latest treatment procedures for prostate cancer

FDA drug approvals for depression indications (www.fda.gov/oashi/depression/cdrug.html)

PharmInfo.com (www.pharminfo.com) a service of

Mediconsultinc.com (www.mediconsultinc.com/)

A Report on the Sponsors of Cancer Treatment Clinical Trials and Their Approval and Monitoring Mechanisms (www.nap.edu/)

Merck Medco (www.merckmedco.com)

Oncolink (www.oncolink.upenn.edu/)

CancerNet (www.cancernet.nci.nih.gov/)

The National Cancer Institute's (NCI) Cancer Net (www.cancernet.nci.nih.gov) - CANCERLTR

Medical Matrix (www.medmatrix.org/index.asp?)

CliniWeb (www.ohsu.edu/cliniweb)

InteliHealth (www.intelihealth.com)

Discovery Health (www.discoveryhealth.com)

Cedar Sinai Medical Center Cancer Group -
(mailto:cancer.web@cshs.org)

Yahoo News (www.yahoo.com) - Updates continuously from
newswires.

Disease information gateways

MEDLINEplus (www.medlineplus.nlm.nih.gov/medlineplus)
(under "Health Topics")
The Karolinska Institute (www.info.ki.se/ki)
Healthgate (www.healthgate.com)
Medical Matrix (www.medmatrix.org)
Healthfinder (www.healthfinder.org/default.htm)
HealthWeb (www.healthweb.org/)
CliniWeb (www.ohsu.edu/cliniweb)
Medsite Navigator (www.medsitenavigator.com/index.html)
NOAH (www.noah.cuny.edu/)
MedWeb (www.cc.emory.edu/WHSCL/medweb.html)
Mayo Clinic Health Oasis (www.mayohealth.org)
Hardin Meta Directory
(www.lib.uiowa.edu/hardin/md/index.html)
Medical World Search (www.mwsearch.com)
HealthAtoZ (www.HealthAtoZ.com)
NLM's PubMed (www.ncbi.nlm.nih.gov/PubMed)
Internet Grateful Med (www.igm.nlm.nih.gov)

Hospitals

Medical-Net's "Hospital Select" (www.hospitalselect.com)-- a reference source of information on individual hospitals in the United State.

AMA Physician Select, On-Line Doctor Finder (www.ama-assn.org/aps/amahg.htm) - gives information concerning the specialists who can treat any specific disaease.

Cedars Sinai Medical Center
(www.csmc.edu/commons/search/sitesearch.htm)

About the Cedars-Sinai Prostate Cancer Center

The Prostate Cancer Center at Cedars-Sinai Medical Center, led by Medical Director Stuart Holden, MD, and Research Director David B. Agus, MD, provides a comprehensive array of cutting-edge treatments for patients with prostate cancer. A state-of-the-art translational research laboratory (dedicated to pre-clinical drug studies) will develop novel therapies for prostate cancer and will support the Center's clinical trials.

The Center is designed to provide a variety of leading-edge treatments to patients with prostate cancer to yield the best possible outcomes.

Managed care coverage

The Health Insurance Association of America (HIAA) (www.hiaa.org) - is a trade association whose members are insurance companies and managed care companies

The Blue Cross and Blue Shield
Association (www.bluescares.com) - provides links to all the
regional associations.

Kaiser Permanente (www.kaiserpermanente.org) - is the largest
not-for-profit health maintenance organization in the country
with 7.5 million members.

Group Health Cooperative of Puget Sound (www.ghc.org) - is
the nation's sixth largest not-for-profit HMO, serving over
700,000 members in the northwestern United States.

The American Association of Health Plans (AAHP)
(www.aahp.org) - This organization represents more than 1,000
HMOs and other network based plans, and serves over 100
million Americans nationwide.

The National Committee for Quality Assurance (NCQA)
(www.ncqa.org) - is an independent, not-for-profit organization
that serves as the accrediting agency for the nation's managed
care plans. NCQA maintains HEDIS 3.0, the standard report
card used to rate and compare managed care plans. Links to
HEDIS 3.0 may be found at the NCQA web site.

The accounting firm Price Waterhouse (www.pwcglobal.com)
maintains an active consulting practice in the managed care
industry. Access survey and research information through their
web site.

Clinical trials

CenterWatch Clinical Trials Listing Service
(www.centerwatch.com) - is a listing of clinical trials.
ClinicalTrials.gov (www.clinicaltrials.gov/ct/gui/c/b)

Search the Studies (www.clinicalstudies.info.nih.gov/)
American College of Physicians (ACP) (www.acponline.org)
Association of Health Care Policy and Research (AHCPR)
(www.ahcpr.gov)
Clinical Trials Search Builder (www.recap.com) - Allows for
the entry of values needed to search the company's database of
biotech Clinical Trials.

Organizations

American Medical Assn. (www.ama-assn.org)
Oncolink (www.oncolink.upenn.edu) (cancer-specific)
CancerNet (www.cancernet.nci.nih.gov) (cancer-specific)
The American Cancer Society (www.cancer.org)
The National Institutes of Health (NIH) (www.nih.gov)
National Cancer Institute (www.nci.nih.gov)
American Psychological Association (www.apa.org)

Journals

JAMA (Journals of the American Medical Assn. at www.ama-
assn.org)
Emory University's MedWeb (www.cc.emory/edu)
New Jour (www.gort.ucsd.edu.newjour/)
University of Texas M.D. Anderson Cancer Center: Medical
Journals Online
(www.mdacc.tmc.edu/~library/Mejoonln/MJOlinks.htm)
MedSite Navigator (www.medsitenavigator.com/med/A.html)

As it turned out, Dr. Steven Roberts' sick uncle was well on the
road to recovery, thanks to his timely participation in a little-
known prostate cancer clinical trial that Tanya Adams had
located.

Also, due to the thorough research that Tanya Adams had performed, Dr. Steven Roberts was able to open his hospital cancer center on time and under budget.

The hospital administrators, along with public health officials raved about the quality, lack of waste, and maximum treatment opportunities for the community's cancer victims.

With the district's senate and congressional representatives present, the mayor held a ceremony to give Dr. Roberts the key to the city.

Tanya was happy for him, but cast her eyes down to the floor, a bit sad that no one knew she did so much of the research that had allowed things to run as smoothly as they did. Suddenly, she heard her name over the P.A. system and looked up.

Dr. Roberts: "Mayor Jenkins, I have to share this key with my new vice president, Tanya Adams. Without her the energy and drive she added by her research work, this center would be much less of the phenomenon that you all recognize it to be."

When everyone, including all of the dignitaries stood and applauded her, Tanya felt woozy.

Dr. Roberts: "Stand up, Ms. Adams. Take a bow."

Tanya held on tight to the back of her chair to steady her wobbling knees. But soon she was standing tall, as she bowed and curtsied to the distinguished crowd.

THE END

Searching Toolchest

Search engines:

HotBot (www.hotbot.com)
AltaVista (www.altavista.com)
Lycos (www.lycos.com)
Northern Light (www.northernlight.com)
AllTheWeb (www.alltheweb.com).
Google (www.google.com)
FAST Search (www.alltheweb.com)
GO/Infoseek (www.go-com)
Inktomi (www.inktomi.com)

Medical-specific search engines
Achoo Healthcare Online (www.achoo.com/main.asp) - in
addition to listings, used to search Medline or the Merck
Manual
CiteLine.com (www.citeline.com)
MedExplorer (www.medexplorer.com)
MedHunt (www.hon.ch/MedHunt)
Medical World Search (www.mwsearch.com) or
(www.enigma.co.nz/mws/mws_source.htm)

Subject directories:

Yahoo! (www.yahoo.com)
Galaxy (www.einet.net/galaxy.html)
Argus Clearinghouse (www.clearinghouse.net)
Submit It! (www.submit-it.com)
LookSmart (www.looksmart.com)
MSN (www.msn.com)
About.com (www.about.com)

Go/Infoseek (www.go.com)
Librarian's Index (www.lii.org)

Directories are easier to use than engines when you need to browse broad subject categories such as news, government, health, etc. and so forth.

Medical subject-specific directories:

HealthWeb (www.healthweb.org)
Medical Matrix (www.medmatrix.org)
MedWeb (www.gen.emory.edu/medweb/medweb.html)
NOAH (www.noah.cuny.edu)
Combined Health Information Database (www.chid.nih.gov)
Healthfinder (www.healthfinder.gov)
CliniWeb (www.ohsu.edu/cliniweb) [(clinical content browsed by Medical Subject Heading (MeSH)].
Hardin Meta Directory of Internet Health Sources: (www.lib.uiowa.edu/hardin/md) (a directory of directories, arranged by medical specialty)
The Comprehensive Health and Medical Index: (www.lib.uiowa.edu/hardin/md/idx.html) (It lists, among other things, reliable directories with established track records for supplying reliable sources of information.)
(Yahoo! Health Information: Web Directories (www.dir.yahoo.com) Health/Web Directories lists over forty of these directories)
HealthSCOUT (www.healthscout.com) - has a search feature for health-related topics. Can give information on diseases, specifics of drug and side effects, etc.

Metasearch gateways (Megasearch portals):

MetaCrawler (www.metacrawler.com)

MetaFind (www.metafind.com)
Mamma (www.mamma.com)
Dogpile (www.dogpile.com)
Inference Find (www.infind.com)
Internet Sleuth (www.isleuth.com)
Copernic (www.copernic.com) (free software download)
The Big Hub (www.thebighub.com)
ProFusion (www.profusion.com)
SavvySearch (www.savvysearch.com)
Highway 61 (www.highway61.com)
Search.com (www.search.com): Unlike most metasearch engines,
this one doesn't just stick to the big names such as AltaVista and Yahoo!
Search.com looks to specialized engines, choosing them for the particular topic you query.
CompletePlanet (www.completeplanet.com) : searches the deep Web to find the right kinds of specialized search sites for the information categories on your mind.

Answer services
Allexperts (www.allexperts.com)
Ask Jeeves (www.askjeeves.com) or (www.ask.com)
Looksmart (www.looksmart.com)
Abuzz (www.abuzz.com)
Askme.com (www.askme.com)
AnswerPoint (www.answerpoint.ask.com)

Miscellaneous tools

The Online Computing Dictionary
(www.InstantWeb.com/foldoc) -
 a simple search engine for technical terms.

Xrefer (www.xrefer.com) - a reference engine for facts, quotes, and words.

ExactOne.com (www.exactone.com) - An engine & "bot" to find services, jobs, books, etc. It can compare prices, shipping schedules and costs, inventory status, etc.

Research-It (www.itools.com/research-it/research-it.html)) - features a Biographical Search section. Type in a person's name, accomplishment or title, and then find the person in the Biographical Dictionary.

AnyWho (www.anywho.com) - type a person or business name, with some location information, to get a phone number. There's also a reverse lookup option so you can type in a phone number to find the person or business behind it. Also possible is a flexible "Begins with" or "Ends with" search that even lets you attempt to trace even a partial phone number.

555-1212.com (www.555-1212.com) - to look up an area code or an entire phone number. It features both Yellow (business) and White (residential) listings for the United States and Canada. It even has some international listings for almost a dozen European countries.

Vicinity (www.vicinity.com) - lets you specify a place in the U.S. or Canada -- by Street, City, State, Province, Zip Code, Area Code -- and a radius from that place -- from 1 to 100 miles. Then you can type details to find a business, service, activity, hospital, museum, restaurant, or summer camp within that circle. (Also available with Northern Lights at (www.northernlight.com/geosearch.html).

Companies Online (www.companiesonline.com) - features listings of more than 100,000 private and public companies. This service gives you the ability to sift through them by using name, ticker symbol, location, and industry.

Fetch O Matic (www.fetchomatic.com) - features a geographic search engine for businesses to hunt through its list of 16 million businesses by name or category. You can make sure the businesses that pop up are within a limited local area or region in the U.S. or Canada, since you also specify a Zip Code or city.

AT&T Help/Search: Directories (www.att.com/directory) - helps you find a person, a business, a phone number, a toll-free number, or a Web site. You can fill in a name, city, zip, phone number, keyword, or other known fact, and search for the unknown fields. The Advanced Search options offer a choice of Begins With, Same As, and Sounds Like to expand the search.

Whois.net (www.whois.net) - shows you who's who among the currently registered 19,826,172 com, net, and org domain names, as well as the 527,792 on hold and the 2,515,087 that have been deleted. Just type the name and click to the organization that owns the domain, along with its address, administrative and technical contacts, and current host servers. If you happen to be interested in using the name for your own work, the contacts include phone numbers and e-mail addresses so that you can learn if the current owners are willing to transfer.

WebShopper (www.webshopper.com) - features PC World Reviews, Buyers Guides, price comparisons and unbiased advice, all in one convenient location.

Consumer health care sites:

NOAH: New York Online Access to Health
(www.noah.cuny.edu)

The Health Care Financing Administration (HCFA)
(www.medicare.gov)
(www.hcfa.gov/news/pr2000/pr001115.htm) - a research tool to
allow consumers to search for information on how to apply for
drug assistance provided by pharmaceutical companies, states,
and community-based programs.

Users can also search using their ZIP codes to receive
information about drug coverage benefits offered by managed
care plans within their community. The HCFA program is
similar to that of PhRMA's RxHope.com, which is supported by
the pharmaceutical industry.

Cancer-specific consumer care sites

Oncolink (www.oncolink.upenn.edu) (cancer-specific)
CancerNet (www.cancernet.nci.nih.gov) (cancer-specific)
The American Cancer Society (www.cancer.org)
The National Institutes of Health (NIH) (www.nih.gov)
National Cancer Institute (www.nci.nih.gov)
Professional health care sites:
CliniWeb (www.ohsu.edu/cliniweb)
InteliHealth (www.intelihealth.com)
Discovery Health (www.discoveryhealth.com)
Medical sites with both professional and consumer orientation:
CancerNet (www.cancernet.nci.nih.gov)
The Centers for Disease Control and Prevention (CDC)
(www.cdc.gov)

Web reference sites:

MEDLINE via PubMed (www.nlm.nih.gov) (a bibliographic database) Harrison's Online (www.harrisononline.com) (medical textbooks) APA Monitor Online: (www.apa.org/monitor/) (full-text journals)

Usenet groups:

Deja News (www.dejanews.com) (Extracts messages from their original groups, reclassifying them into more meaningful divisions. Included under Health is a broad range of topics: Diseases and Disorders, Children's Health, Women's Health, etc.).

Tile.Net (www.tile.net/lists/medicine.html) - is a directory of listservs and usenet newsgroups.

Liszt, The Mailing List Directory (www.Liszt.com) - provides links to usenet newsgroups.

E-mail discussion lists:

Research-It (www.itools.com/research-it/research-it.html) - includes a search feature for Listservs. If you want to see which e-mail discussion groups include a topic of interest, just enter that topic here, and click to look it up.

Tile.net (www.tile.net/lists)
Publicly Accessible Mailing Lists
(www.neosoft.com/internet/paml)

Liszt, The Mailing List Directory (www.Liszt.com) - is a search tool that specializes in locating listservs.

Newsgroups

Remarq (www.remarq.com) - can help to search for one of the 30,000 Newsgoups that are on the Internet, but not on the World Wide Web.

Domain name registry agencies

- Look up the domain registry page at the appropriate registry agency:
- For .com, .edu, .net, .org : http://www.networksolutions.com/cgi-bin/whois/whois
- For .gov (U.S. government) : http://www.nic.gov/cgi-bin/whois
- For .mil (U.S. military) : http://www.nic.mil/cgi-bin/whois
- For Asian-Pacific : http://www.apnic.net/apnic-bin/whois.pl
- For European : http://www.ripe.net/cgi-bin/whois

The rest of the world: http://www.uninett.no/navn/domreg.html

Final Exercise

Now try applying what you have learned to some questions about eye surgery:

Regarding the trustworthiness of Internet medical information: Which of the following sentences is not true regarding the results of a search for optical device manufacturers?
A. One should always carefully evaluate the information obtained on a Web site before using it.
B. There is no need to consult a doctor if you can just get medical information from a Web site.
C. Every medicine-oriented Web site is harmful.
Answer: B.

In searching for medical information (such as eye laser manufacturers), people who have a significant amount of search experience typically start by:
A. Familiarizing themselves with one of the specialized medical or health subject directories.
B. Conducting a metasearch for "eye laser manufacturers."
C. Submitting a query to a general search engine, such as Google for "eye laser manufacturers."
Answer: A.

Which of the following search statements does not use one of the Boolean logic operators?
A. cataract AND implant surgery
B. cataract OR implant surgery
C. cataract AND NOT implant surgery
D. cataract LESS THAN implant surgery
Answer: D.

In troubleshooting a search for "laser eye surgery equipment sales" that returns far too many documents, what can you do?
A. Use less common words, that is, find synonyms (e.g. "PRK" or "LASIK").
B. Try adding at least two more specific terms to your string to narrow down the search results (e.g., vision correction).
C. Use Boolean operators to pinpoint the search (+laser~eye~surgery)
D. All of the above.
Answer: D.

Which of the following is NOT a good way to start the search for disease information, such as for glaucoma or cataracts?
A. Look at known sites of quality on the subject.
B. Look at every possible site regarding human diseases.

C. Visit general medical sites that specialize in organizing and providing information.
D. Locate the site of an organization that states a mission to provide information on that disease.
Answer: B.